The Apocalyptic
MANNEQUIN

The definition of body is buried

Stephanie M.
Wytovich

RAW DOG
SCREAMING
PRESS

The Apocalyptic Mannequin ©2019 by Stephanie M. Wytovich

Published by Raw Dog Screaming Press
Bowie, MD

First Edition

Cover illustration: Steven Archer
Book design: M. Garrow Bourke

ISBN: 978-1-947879-13-3

Printed in the United States of America

www.RawDogScreaming.com

Previously published

Unnerving Magazine. "Beneath the Rubble, They're Watching." Print. 2017.

HWA Poetry Showcase. "The Apocalyptic Mannequin." Print. 2017.

Literary Hatchet. "Hospital Notes Written on the Gauze for My Sores." Print. 2017.

Clash Media. "Behind the Genetic Reaping" "Nuclear Test Site: Round 2," and "Radiation Poisoning and Stale Coffee for Breakfast." Online. 2017.

Not One of Us Digest. "Return to Womb" Print. 2017.

Crystal Lake Publishing. Tales from the Lake, Vol. 5. "From the Mouths of Plague-Mongers. Print. 2018.

The Pedestal Magazine. "The Survival of Fishes." Web. 2018

Smart Rhino Publications. A Plague of Shadows. "A Hanger in the World of Dance." Print. 2018.

Post Mortem Press. She's Lost Control. "Dinner Time: The Consequences of Savages." Print. 2018.

Star*Line Magazine. "Nearsighted in the Mushroom Cloud." Print. 2018

Sanitarium Magazine. "Corpse-Covered Glasses." Web. 2018.

Unnerving. Haunted Are These Houses. "Our Room of Walking Coffins." Print. 2018.

Dissections. "At the Neon Circus." Web. 2019.

Gallows Hill. "Cannibalism: A Robot Anachronism." Web. 2019.

StokerCon 2019 Souviner Anthology. "Return to Sender." Print. 2019.

Also by Stephanie M. Wytovich

Poetry
Hysteria: A Collection of Madness
Mourning Jewelry
An Exorcism of Angels
Brothel
Sheet Music to My Acoustic Nightmare

Novel
The Eighth

Advance Praise

"Like a doomsday clock fast-forwarding to its final self-destruction, Wytovich's poetry will give you whiplash as you flip through page after page. The writing here is ugly yet beautiful. It reads like a disease greedily eating up vital organs. The apocalypse has arrived and it couldn't be more intoxicating!" —Max Booth III, author of *Carnivorous Lunar Activities*

"In this hauntingly sensuous new collection of poetry, you'll long to savor every apocalyptic nightmare you have ever feared. Blooming in the beauty of destruction and the terror of delight, Stephanie M. Wytovich's poems remind us that we feel the world better, love the world better, when we recognize the ephemeral nature of everything achingly alive beyond our mannequin minds. Here, we are captive to our deepest velvet snarls, zombie songs, and radioactive wishes, at the mercy of a neon reaping. Reading this collection is like dancing through Doomsday, intoxicated by the destructive, decadent truth of desire in our very mortality. In these poems, you will find revelry in the ruins of everything you once held dear — and you will love it to the last as you watch the world unravel around you."—Saba Syed Razvi, author of *Heliophobia* and *In the Crocodile Gardens*

"Beautifully bleak, Stephanie M. Wytovich's latest collection posits scenarios of the apocalypse and the horrors to come thereafter with language like fragrant hooks in your skin. Vivid, each word a weight on your tongue, these poems taste of metal and ash with a hint of spice, smoke. She reminds us the lucky ones die first, and those who remain must face the horrors of a world painted in blisters and fear. Leave it to Wytovich to show us there's beauty in the end, just beneath all that peeling, irradiated skin."
—Todd Keisling, author of *Ugly Little Things* and *Devil's Creek*

"Set in a post-apocalyptic world that at times seems all too near, Wytovich's poems conjure up frighteningly beautiful and uncomfortably prescient imagery. Populated by a cast of unsettling, compelling characters, this collection is one that stuck with me."
—Claire C. Holland, author of *I Am Not Your Final Girl*

"A surreal journey through an apocalyptic wasteland, a world that is terrifyingly reminiscent of our own even as the blare of evacuation alarms drowns out the sizzle of acid rain, smiling mannequins bear witness to a hundred thousand deaths, and "the forest floor grows femurs in the light of a skeletal moon." Stephanie M. Wytovich's *The Apocalyptic Mannequin* is as unsettling as it is lovely, as grotesque as it is exquisite."
—Christa Carmen, author of *Something Borrowed, Something Blood-Soaked*

The Apocalyptic
MANNEQUIN

The definition of body is buried

Contents

Author's Note: -- 15

Eat the Breath of the Apocalypse ------------------------------------- 17

Behind the Genetic Reaping-- 18

Greetings from the New World --- 19

When the World Began to Swell ------------------------------------- 20

It's in the Rain -- 21

Nearsighted in the Mushroom Cloud-------------------------------- 22

Radiation Poisoning and Stale Coffee for Breakfast ---------------- 23

To Bear Witness -- 24

Ground Zero-- 25

Viral-- 27

Plagued --- 28

Beneath the Rubble, They're Watching ----------------------------- 29

Nuclear Test Site: Round 2 -- 30

Underland -- 31

Small Suffocations-- 32

There's No Air Left -- 33

The Evacuation Rally--- 34

Everything Must End --- 36

Please Stand By--- 37

The Silencing-- 38

Without Light -- 39

When the Snow Falls Black-- 40

Under the Morningstar's Watch -------------------------------------- 41

Remaking Eve--- 42

Madam, Never Mistress-- 43

Saints Don't Spread Their Legs --------------------------------------- 44

Warnings in the Suicide Forest --------------------------------------- 45

The Second Coming -- 46

Without the Gas Mask -- 47

Forest of Femurs-- 48

Mounted-- 49

A Hanger in The World of Dance ------------------------------- 50

Underneath Atomic Lake --------------------------------------51

The Survival of Fishes--- 52

The Amputator's Flesh Fry ----------------------------------- 53

Future Mannequins on Display -------------------------------- 54

Dead People Down Here--- 55

Abandonment--- 56

Lost Highways --57

What They Left Behind --- 58

Only What Could Be Carried ---------------------------------- 59

Those Little Sacrifices--- 60

This, the Sound of Begging ----------------------------------61

Trapped Inside-- 62

Cannibalized --- 63

Saudade--- 64

A Collection of Pomegranate Seeds-------------------------- 65

Return to Sender --- 66

Hospital Notes Written on the Gauze for My Sores---------------- 67

I Walk Nowhere in Cities Long Past Dead -------------------- 68

Dinner Time: The Consequences of Savages ----------------- 69

Cannibalism: A Robot Anachronism ------------------------71

From the Mouths of Plague-Mongers -------------------------- 72

The Manufacturing of Bodies -------------------------------- 73

The Apocalyptic Mannequin----------------------------------- 74

At the Neon Circus ---75

All Things Poison -- 76

Marionette Disorder--77

The Mannequin Legs on My Bed ---------------------------- 78

Walking on Teeth: A Memoir ----------------------------------- 79

Our Room of Walking Coffins---------------------------------- 80

Wayward Spirits of Dreams and Sand-------------------------------81

Mirror Gazing-- 82

Of Sleeping Witches Woken ----------------------------------- 84

For I Am a Woman Made of Snakes --------------------------- 85

The Stones They Threw -------------------------------------- 86

Inside the House of Labor ----------------------------------- 87

What Mother Couldn't Tell You------------------------------ 88

From Maiden to Monster ------------------------------------ 89

Scavenger--- 90

Woman Meat---91

Still Life with Scars --- 92

As the Crow Flies --- 93

Identification --- 94

Call Me Haunted-- 95

Return to Womb -- 96

Corpse-Covered Glasses ------------------------------------- 97

A Spectacle of Corpses -------------------------------------- 98

The Collection Day Saints ----------------------------------- 99

Consumption's Footprint------------------------------------100

Gather the Townspeople------------------------------------- 101

The Midwives of Death-------------------------------------- 102

Dear Santa Muerte --- 103

Corpse Meditation --- 105

The Martyrdom of Saints ----------------------------------- 106

I Bury Them Screaming------------------------------------- 107

Open Casket--108

Death Bed ---109

Eating What's Left of My Death------------------------------ 110

A Masquerade of Reapers------------------------------------111

For Dennis.
Until the end of the world.
And then some.

Author's Note:

WHEN I THINK ABOUT WHAT scares me lately, it's being cheated out of time and having my home, my family and friends, all those delicious possibilities and opportunities in life taken away from me too early and without my say. My fears also live in the loss of my rights and my freedom to do and say and go as I please, and so I stay up at night, losing sleep, getting angry, all while praying that day won't be today, that it won't be tomorrow…that it [and it is a wealth of endless horrors that we probably can't even begin to imagine] won't happen at all.

As such, this book is my apocalypse cry, my doomsday preparation list. I hope that it's a collection of nightmares, but the reality is that some of the monsters are getting bigger and stronger these days, so this book is also a petition, a fight song. It's a reminder of past disasters, of current tragedies. A warning about the future we carve out for ourselves.

So read these poems and hold your loved ones close. Use your voice to stand up for others, and when/if you see someone who needs help, who needs evacuated, who needs a drink of fresh water or the comfort of a warm meal, open your heart and your homes to help them.

Because in the end, we're all in this together.

And no one should have to go through this alone.

—Stephanie M. Wytovich
June 12, 2019

Eat the Breath of the Apocalypse

In the event of cigarettes lit by nuclear explosions,
I will stand naked in my burning, the thoughts of
broken porcelain and worms in my mouth
the safety net I need to climb into bed at night.

Tell me: does the sight of dissection scare you? Let me
show you my throat, how it swallows discarded
receipts and digital footprints, the way my stomach
acid dissolves Twitter handles and retweets like
rotten, pre-chewed food.

I think the smoke in my lungs has killed the host
family living inside of me. Can you turn up the music
to Doomsday? I would dance, but I can't feel my skin,
these bones are like paper, like eyelashes flapping in the wind.

Outside the trees are melting. My car is idle,
its tires slashed, its horn removed. In the distance
the screams of gods filter through my radio,
their feasts a reminder of why I eat the breath
they wasted on my birth.

Behind the Genetic Reaping

The world, a soon-to-be hospice,
brings with it a creature, a monster,
a culmination of everything less-than-desired,
an inactive participant, dormant, asleep;
yet there's a stewing in the after-wake of medical nightmare,
this freak-show discovery,
this harbinger of mutation,
it waits in syringes-induced comas
hesitates in its failed posthumous abortion
for inside this genetic accident,
there exists the hardship of weakness,
an off-color, misbranded creation
that looks different than those around it;
a blinking taboo, a wheezing unmentionable
there's a crack in the system, a fracture in the plan

But, hear me, death-bed inhabitants!
Listen close: there's a reaper in your head.

A slave to the dominance of survival,
there's a cowering, a receding back to black,
a hanging in its suspended womb, this miscarriage-survived;
it was created to suffer, to duel out the agony of existence,
to force feed humanity its political agenda of hate;
like a well-oiled mechanical mutant,
it writhes in declination with each breath,
a recessive abomination, disease-ridden and paled,
it feasts on your supply of white blood cells and hope,
a meat suit siphoned, a psychic heretic
it will eat you to survive, harvest you to laugh.

Greetings from the New World

The first blast popped my ear drum, its sound like
gunfire in my head; I didn't open my eyes for three days,
couldn't breathe without wondering if that air would be my last,
if the taste of metal would ever leave my mouth.

I boarded up windows, nailed the doors shut, but mostly,
I got used to darkness, got used to their screaming,
their gnawing and desperation, how they begged
to be let in, each plea a curse, a velvet-coated lie.

It was weeks before I first saw them, how they
threw their bodies against the door, bashed their heads
against the kitchen windows, their hands like bloody
fillets slapping against glass as they fed, each slaughter
a mockery of my unwillingness, every murder a reminder
of what happens when warm flesh meets the new world.

When the World Began to Swell

The ground shook, cracked like dry skin
when the gas escaped, floated up in the sky
like a quiet green whisper. Leaves fell from trees,
their bodies like parachutes, like angel wings
feathering down to the floor in autumnal blankets.

It's been months since the fumes, since the jade
smoke hit the air. Bodies grew in their graves,
their eyes like great balloons, these floating
dismembered observers with plump, distended
torsos popping from too much pressure.

It smelled like spoiled beef, the earth wet
like rotten vegetables, everything dripping,
everything damp. Bluebirds swelled to the size
of rabbits, dropped from the sky like multicolored bombs,
their necks cracked, their bones broken, everything
two, three, four times its size, this the monstrous
growing of a dying, bloated world.

It's in the Rain

Locked in the bunker, the metal walls
a reminder of a tired reflection, the hazmat
suit hanging on the coat rack like a warning
sign, begging me to reconsider, to die a safe
death, one absent of the pain of knowing,
the screaming outside still too much to bear.

Did you know how fast the flesh can be
consumed? How quickly tears can turn to blood,
little splashes of death that litter the body, eating
it like a starved hyena, laughing at our attempt
to fight? When the storm came, it came without
warning, without explanation. Radios shut down,
signals got lost, the earth swallowed the life
it once birthed, now a ravenous mother eager
for the bones of her children.

I watched from my castle underground, saw
the water enter their mouths, the vomit
a bright blue ocean of disease. It worked fast,
how it stripped their flesh, liquefied their eyes,
this tsunami of corpses like rafts floating
through the forest, their bloated stares
a cinematic frame.

Sometimes, I wonder what it feels like, how the rain
sinks into the face, the neck, the arms: if it burns,
if it freezes, the body an incubator for the virus,
the bacteria that strips and eats, discards and buries;
but outside, the rain is getting harder, the water flooding
the city, each road an underwater village, each town a
dilapidated Atlantis, but I make peppermint tea in my kitchen,
smile at the way they all used to laugh, at the way I prepped
and planned, speculated and conspired, for the time is now,
and it is I who survives.

Nearsighted in the Mushroom Cloud

When I breathe, the air pierces my lungs,
A subtle attack against my attempt to survive,
This knife wound in my chest, it pulsates
throbbing and festering, the maggots of my infection
A reminder that we are nothing but spoiled meat.

I don't know when it first started,
When the outside became poison, a neon tonic
To drink down in our gasmask couture, but I cower
Amongst the rotted leaves and apple cores,
my jean jacket ripped, my gloves, fingerless;
there's no home to go back to, the world before
now a distant memory filled with trivialities like hope.

How did I miss seeing the world die?
Was I nearsighted in the mushroom cloud?
Blinded by the smoke, the billowing fog
That licked me ash, its tongue a cumulus assault
Trailing down my back?

All these little deaths, they come in quiet jabs,
The suffocation of cells, the amputations of limbs
I wear their marks like collages on my skin,
This tableau of pain, a futile assassination attempt
To kill something that's already died.

But there aren't funerals for girls who still walk,
No time for melancholia when your skin is ripped open,
A culmination of green pustules swimming in pockmarked flesh;
I swallow my teeth sometimes, try to convince myself
That my nails are not food, but I bite my cuticles, suck the dirt
From my palms, and every morning when the sun doesn't rise,
I pray to Lucifer that whatever Hell he's building, he
Finishes it soon.

Radiation Poisoning and Stale Coffee for Breakfast

My coffee cup is teal, bought on a whim when I found there were others,
The threadbare blanket on my sofa will have to do
Much like the food that expires today, but it's still good,
I promise—trust me like you did the day the stars stopping shining

Because when I open the mailbox, there's a letter from two years ago,
Left still, dead like the time I wandered into the forest,
All those hallucinogenic colors dripping from branches,
Making impressions in the pond.

There is a haunting in the wind now, the sound like crying wasps,
Their wings broken, stilted in a proverbial twitch, I feel the prick
Of a thousand stingers inside me, my lungs filled with radiation,
The world glowing like the first time I dropped acid.

Here, take a seat, this bone marrow will make you strong,
Let me grab you a cup of soup from the sky's tears,
It's been weeping all morning, the Big Dipper is bored
Sometimes when I'm lonely, I remember out back,
I've already dug up my own grave.

To Bear Witness

Collapsed eyeballs dripped like candlewax on the table, an almost-blink, a fractured wink, they sat and watched the outside world combust, each puff of smoke a cancer, every poisonous cloud a fog to strip away the hope that remained.

Ground Zero

Beneath the soil of radioactive craters,
there's a whispering, a shudder of air
still warm from the blast, its breath
a death note, an incurable disease
begging to be inhaled.

> Fear its body: the way it stands tall,
> invisible, a mirage that wields
> your DNA like a serrated knife
> against a calf's throat.

> *Is it inside you yet?*

Because it will call to you first,
taunt you with its glow, a neon wink
against a desert rose, this taste an oasis
buried in the bodies of disfigured corpses,
their tongues, a burnt family portrait,
their eyes, a dripping kitchen sink.

> Walk carefully: each step
> is a dusting with death, a chance
> to lick the air that killed hundreds,
> to taste the heat that brought them
> screaming and begging to their knees.

> *Can you still hear them?*

The children of mushroom clouds
are laughing, their voices like smoke,
like cancer and baby teeth, a clattering
of bone meal and unanswered prayers
left hanging in the wind.

Stephanie M. Wytovich

Listen close: their obituaries float
overhead like misshapen torsos,
like deformed hands unable, but
determined, to grab.

Do they have you yet?

Viral

Could you taste the poison when you stole the axe from the shed, when you pulled the blinds down and asked us what we wanted for our birthdays, like we had a list, like we thought another year would bring back the scent of trick candles and Mom baking in the kitchen.

I have a migraine and I think my name is Viral, but the bite marks in my head are clouding my memory and the fish swimming behind my eyes make me crave salty instead of sweet.

Did you know that listening to screaming makes me nostalgic for when you used to take us to playgrounds, a handful of candy in my pocket instead of nails, instead of tongues, nothing like today where currency is a weeping sore, a neon bruise, pumping, pulsing, pounding…

There's a buzzing in my ears and when I try to talk, my jaw droops, falls off in my hands, but somehow that doesn't matter because my spit is pooling and people are running.

Is there a place that's safe for people like us, the ones who exist in blood-stained tissues and calloused hands, the dirt under my fingernails a mixture of organ and mud, their bodies collecting, piling, gathering, each limb a fork, every torso the dining room table our family eats on.

Plagued

It tasted like millipedes and firewood,
all that crunching, the way smoke tended
to get stuck in your teeth. I felt it in my
throat first, a tickle, an itch, something
like a spider crawling out of your mouth,
its eyes like windows to the virus brewing,
calculating inside.

I didn't know I was bleeding until I wiped
my nose, until I coughed up blood, charcoal,
the red-black smack of phlegm hard against
my teeth. It smelled like sickness, the way
my neighbor smelled before she died: rotten,
sour, like a piece of leftover meat sitting
too long in the sun.

It only took hours before my skin
started to slip. I peeled it like an orange,
slowly at first. I collected the rinds in
mason jars, my muscles adapting like
memory foam to the stale slap of air.

It's hard to say when I went blind
because at some point, I feel asleep,
my body wrapped in towels, blood thick
on my hands, my jaundiced skin reflecting
off the glass of water I could no longer drink,
my tongue dried up and crumbled, swallowed
like an after-dinner mint.

Beneath the Rubble, They're Watching

The ground is aflame with the ends of tomorrows
its doomsday flowers wilted, petals like seared flesh.
The sky, blanketed in smoke, wears its nightcap,
sleeps in the ever dark that cloaks the earth
while an unbound silence whispers
to a child's headless doll against the glow
of a fallen star.

Beneath the rubble, they're watching us
laughing at our sores, our brittle broken bones.
Can you feel them? Does the sound of their plastic
bodies rub against the inside of your mouth, claw at
the canals in your ears?

Our gasmask couture filters out their poison,
keeps the ash off our faces, but if you breathe in the venom,
if you savor the sweet, cloying toxins in the air,
you'll find the screams of radiations past, all those
mushroom-cloud pillows and forgotten mannequin smiles;
They'll wrap you up in their apocalyptic charm,
their marble eyes stoic against the clamor of
hustling limbs.

Left behind, discarded, they are the risen now,
the ones who survived, the stitched and the flayed,
their bodies meat to the starving earth, a prime-cut
sacrifice made unwilling before its time. If you listen,
the wind holds stories about a time when the world was young,
hopeful, not burning the promise from yesterday's mouth,
but these creatures, half-human, half-doll,
are all that's left to savage the tombs we made.

Nuclear Test Site: Round 2

The second time, nothing came back but roaches stained smoke and ash
against the backdrop of a gray desert and a yellow-mushroom sky. They raced toward
the demolition camp, past feral refugees buried underground in shelters made of
wood and wreckage, their bodies mutated, their screams a faint howl in the stillborn air.

A moaning,
A weeping,

Droids tracked the homes for carnage: four pairs of goggles, the traumatized
    hands of a test dummy,
a torso made of wires, a torn suit and sheared apron. The fake family's paper dinner
still glued to the kitchen table. The door of a microwave unhinged, propped against
    the sink
inside the seventh identical house in the site.

A blasting,
A shattering,

There's no clean-up, just abandonment, this leaving of all things mattered at
    the cost of science,
at the price of war. An atomic experiment, a nuclear trial. The robots collect
    pressed soil from holes
large enough to house prehistoric monsters, test air poisoned enough to wilt
    the metal of their eyes,
to choke the electricity from their chests.

The Apocalyptic Mannequin

Underland

Running through fields full of landmines,
the air thick with smoke, with the ash of 666
burning trees, I fall down thirteen flights of
rabbit holes, sleep in crop circles in Chernobyl's
playground, the sing-song lullabies of mutated flesh
and deformed bodies the missing security blanket I
kept reaching for, the crackle of the fires, the explosion
of the bombs, the white noise machine that puts me to sleep.

Small Suffocations

A magician's secret, an invisible man,
he walked the towns like a ghost, a quiet
poltergeist disrupting the lives of all who
lived there, their deaths soft, noiseless, a
small suffocation stumbling into the street.

There's No Air Left

There is blood spatter mixing with the herbs in my tea,
the ones I picked that morning before you started to cough,
to hack like a sharpened axe moving into a tree, an airy
blunt-force trauma, violent with a steel bite.

I remember when I didn't have to wear a face mask,
when I could breathe full and with an open mouth,
suck in air the way teenagers forget to when they kissed,
all those sloppy beginnings now riddled with virus,
a time bomb ticking underneath our tongues.

If there was a way to bring you back, to heal the sores
multiplying on your chest, restore the color to your face,
I would wrestle the sweat-soaked bedsheets off your body,
lick the sickness from your eyes, but it's getting harder
to breathe with my throat closing up and there's no air left
to tell you goodbye.

Stephanie M. Wytovich

The Evacuation Rally

The alarms came first, the world
one blinking red light. Emergency
vibrated on the tips of every tongue,
each go bag filled with photographs
and distilled water, granola and Advil.

I put boards against my front door,
painted the windows black, hoarded batteries
as if they were diamonds. At night, I burned
candles in the basement, just enough to keep
the shadows and shrieks at bay, my laundry
stained sweat and paranoia, my kitchen, a host
of broken plates and flies, spoiled meat and mold.

During the day, I watched blood drip
from the cracks in the doors, all those
broken fists banging and pleading,
their voices the sound of sickness,
each cough a broken rib, each sneeze
a busted blood vessel. I hum the lullabies
I would have sung to my firstborn; I stopped
praying to be saved, the solitude its own
death sentence behind these walls.

That afternoon, when the gun shots rained,
I laid on the floor, the linoleum never cold,
my hands placed on the back of my head

waiting, waiting, waiting

for the signal, the evacuation rally. I never leave
but the men never stop trying to save me, this
the home of my dead, the place I was born,
the place I was infected. I pick my jawbone

The Apocalyptic Mannequin

off the floor and slink into the bathroom,
my reflection the murder they wrote each
day as they kill my family trying to return.

How long will it last, this the caterpillar
inside the cocoon? When I make my entrance,
will they marvel at my wings, or will they,
like they did to so many others, tear them from my back
and set my corpse on fire?

Everything Must End

The radio spits static, the mumbled words like white noise
against the mattress I kept in the bed of my truck, the sounds
of wooden crosses and freshly dug graves the swan songs
left trapped and singing in the trees.

Outside of town, the billboard said 'pray,' a sick joke told
from the mouths of corpses, the empty silence of playgrounds
a reminder of when the teeth took the children, when the earth
shook and the waters rose, the eye of the storm a raging god
from a world left forgotten in the sea.

You can still taste the salt in the air, still feel the crispness
of the waves about to break, but when the sirens blare at dusk
and the bodies of sharks and fish are thrown lifeless to the shore,
there is only one certainty in this world, and the ink
that stains your hands is proof of it.

Please Stand By

The television went to static, each channel
a group of wiggling maggots, their white bodies
gyrating on the screen in a parasitic orgy while
sirens screamed through the town, a dying banshee
raking her nails against our throats.

There weren't any signs, no locusts or darkness,
but when they came, they came in hordes, the blood
of my neighbors ballooning against my windows,
their limbs beating against the door in a symphony
of violent acts.

I stood by, I watched, my legs cemented in fear,
pins and needles burrowing in my hands, but the sound,
the sound of their black lips smacking, how their jaws,
a massacre of fangs, went on for days as they fell from sky,
leapt from the trees, their bodies tense as a coil of rope,
their eyes hungry, desperate to feed, as they made
contact with my own, two headlights on a lonely road.

It wasn't long before they were on me, swift like arsenic,
their fists banging against the door, each claw a premeditated
knife wound, this the filleting of my body, the breaking news
never to air because here, in this tomb, there are no headlines,
no cover stories. I am a lost signal, a Jane Doe, and here,
they're just bodies, bodies and the new death.

The Silencing

Their bridges are built on star dust and dead skin,
the crash sites a placeholder, a reminder of cites burned,
of flesh taken, all those whispers of existence
leaked out by cut throats now silenced, their bodies
left bleeding and empty in a mockery of fields.

Without Light

Like tar slipped into my eyes,
the world grew into a blackness,
an ink spot, this culmination of
raven feathers dusted tourmaline,
painted oil, all those charcoal-kissed
butterflies drowning in the open,
their wings heavy, weighed down
with the arms of night.

      It seemed so long ago, and yet my candles
      don't catch, the matches never spark;

And when I step outside, I am bathed
in a blackberry wine, the air a silent
sob, the weeping veil of a widow in
mourning. Every shadow is a plague
mask, a dripping, oozing, sore punctured
from the horns of monsters.

      I cover myself in gasoline, and yet my teeth
      never burn, my body won't ignite.

Stephanie M. Wytovich

When the Snow Falls Black

In mounds made of ashes and bones,
I breathe the air of revelations, drop to my knees,
the blood of our sins raging red rivers through the streets,
a holocaust of rage and locusts, the horseman ride
hungry, savage, their appearance like trumpets sounding songs
of hail and fire, the earth burning, burning, burning
like broken seals, like disconnected sigils. There's no
running, no forgiveness.

We all meet the dragon tonight.

Under the Morningstar's Watch

Smoke fills my mouth in long gray snakes,
their tails coiling in my throat like a witch's knot,
delicate and binding while twin scorpions burrow
behind my eyes, their poison a hallucinogen,
a taste of lightning before the storm.

I choke back laughter as visions of fire encase me,
as leaves dance around the circle, my naked flesh
writhing against the smell of pine and earth. It hurts,
all this burning, how these waves of celestial chaos
churn inside me, ripping, tearing, the fangs of the
wolf digging into my wrists, my blood running
hot, igniting the dance of wailing women
under the Morningstar's watch.

But we continue to gather, to choke down the air
of silenced throats, to collect the bones left by
angry men from beaten women, this the tomb,
the womb of our sisters, a burial ground
of snapped necks and cursed tongues: feed us,
believe us, we're here to do your work.

Remaking Eve

With confidence, they moved like two full moons, a blossoming rebirth
in a city full of poison and blood. Hear them as they feed, their laugh
a snake charmer's kiss, this the black parade of revelations revised:
can you feel the fire around your waist, the breath of the dragon
on your tongue?

The bells are ringing, the skies breaking, each water drop
an open wound, every whisper a coffin lowered into the ground,
its wood splintered, its corpse screaming. There were moments
when it felt like dying was a gift, but the stake we're tied to
doesn't reflect the witchcraft in the air, all those reversed prayers
that sound like the snapped necks of successful hangings,
our bent-neck stares a curse, a promise.

But like martyrs, we let them work, our flesh the fire, our ashes
the beds of a new garden, a new generation. Watch as we regrow
our sisterhood, a rib from our rib, the scent of apple seeds in our
hair. With drowned lungs and dead eyes, we'll emerge from the earth,
the tree of knowledge growing in our wombs, for we are the chosen,
we are the coven, and this is how we'll remake Eve.

Madam, Never Mistress

The locusts slam against the glass, their wings vibrating,
a constant slap while you push inside me, the screams
of sin rallying in the distant, all that bloodlust and fire,
the smoke fills my lungs.

It's the third time you've visited me since the falling,
the imprint of your hooves still visible on my throat,
the rut in full bloom, you rack your horns against my back,
mark me silent, brand me feral; but it was my choice,
this contract—madam never mistress:

> I bow to no one,
> especially you.

Saints Don't Spread Their Legs

See how I hold myself, the way my bones are silent, stiff
despite the breaks. I've been standing broken for months,
a cracked nesting doll, a scapegoat left to rot, all those nights
of calculated silence, of terrified stillness, each breath a risk,
my lungs praying, pleading, filled with rosaries and cement.

I stopped drinking holy water at fourteen, told my father
that the knives in my back made it hard to sleep, how the
visions in my head brought locusts in my room, their chirps
a reminder that with spread legs and evil thoughts, my body,
my chapel was constantly being watched.

At eighteen, mother told me that ladies died without sin,
that purity in the face of evil would be rewarded, my sisters
all saints, all mutilated virgins, their chastity a prize above the slits
in their throats, how they dripped wine like sacrament while I slid
into the garden, lost myself amongst the snakes and vines,
each whisper a blasphemy, every orgasm a crime against God.

See, I was supposed to die like the others, my flesh ripped,
my head torn from my body, but this newfound church
of desire and moans spoke profanity in the face of the cross,
and while my sisters sleep in graves, I stand on freedom,
beaten and broken, forever weathering the storm,
each night an awakening, a chance to be reborn.

The Apocalyptic Mannequin

Warnings in the Suicide Forest

A pinch of salt chased with rainwater,
I swallowed the hauntings of lost ropes
and ribbons, the hanging limbs of cracked
branches and left-behind tents, all those
echoing footsteps and last-minute whispers
food for the yurei, their quiet movements
a ground-born fog over twisted roots and
treacherous trees.

There's a bareness in this sea of foliage,
a claustrophobia born out of too much space:
if you listen carefully, you'll hear
a lingering discomfort brought on by crimes
of ubasute, their thirst-soaked wheezes a whisper
in the calm air against discarded backpacks,
empty bottles of pills.

Tape the trees in strips of blue and yellow,
it's easy to be seduced, the curiosity
of the forest too much for most: a pile
of bones, a littering of clothes.

When the canopy darkens, the howls
trapped in caves release, each leaf
a sitting demon, a patient ghost, watching,
waiting, pleading for you to lose your way,
for you to get curious, for you to take just one step
off the carefully curated path.

The Second Coming

Against the willow tree, its branches long, twisted,
a place where nooses like to grow, I drank the dew
of mornings past, savored the soaked moonlight left
pooling in the dirt.

I screamed for years, the death of my sisters too strong,
too fresh, the stench of burning, the taste of ash
still lingering in the air like black magic, like bedlam
from men whose words bit harder, whose knives dug
deeper, their laughter a sharpened scythe against our cries.

But here in these woods, locked inside this canopy of chaos,
a new breed of woman is born, one who sings with wolves,
her voice the tarot spread against the darkness, the hidden
chasm of energy suckled from jimsonweed and mushrooms,
a harvest unto herself, she is sunrise and death, both casket
and newborn babe.

Listen to her malice, to the chill moving through your teeth,
this the birthplace of my family's home, a gathering of circles
fostered out of blood-born sacrifice, the footsteps
of those before me still walking into the trees, their spirits
forever painting the lips of those who damned them,
who marked and maimed the flesh of women
who had not yet signed the book, their blood still virgin,
their deaths too soon.

But now in this clearing, now against these odds,
the maiden becomes the mother becomes the crone becomes
the night, and all those left hanging, all those left burned,
will rise and dance in her glory, this the second coming,
the rebirth of Eve.

The Apocalyptic Mannequin

Without the Gas Mask

The trees of my hometown run together
their leaves blurred in a forest fire, hot like
bombs, like the taste of metal on my tongue.

Forest of Femurs

Littered with calcium and blossoms of collagen,
the forest floor grows femurs in the light of skeletal moons,
each pocket a whimsical shank, every chamber a canal
of fossilized cancer, arthritic canals.

They stand like soldiers extending into stars,
their desiccated blood vessels like mute wind chimes
in the breeze, a small touch of death in the flapping
of split arteries and sallow shards, they are jungle gyms
of deserters and escapees, the remains of their bones
a children's game, plucked piece by piece
like porcelain petals.

Mounted

I didn't realize how long I'd been standing there
until its antlers were in my stomach, its breath
hot on my skin. It pushed me, pinned me, the trunk
of an old oak tree my prison, my body now complete
with bars.

> With a black tongue, it lapped at the blood,
> its hooves digging into the ground, its eyes
> wild, absent, lost in ritual as it dug in deeper,
> my ribs, it's crown.

Λ Hanger in The World of Dance

It's cold amongst these corpses
I don't belong here, not with them,
The life-takers, the body-huskers

Why won't they stop staring?
Their swollen eyes like skies of gibbous moons…

My spirit screams
They stuff leaves in my mouth,
Shove twigs under my nails

They lick lips with swollen, rubbery tongues,
Their broken spines like knives…

I didn't ask for this death
Sometimes I can still hear father weeping,
Feel his fingertips in my hair

Their breath smells like crying
Such stale, stagnant air…

There was rope, chaffing
They spun me in circles,
Clapped as I choked

Their teeth like cracked pearls,
Their mouths twisted in stitched-on smiles…

At night, I hear the suicides moan,
They sing hymns about release
I cry songs about life

They celebrate this welcoming,
Strip me naked, teach me how to dance…

The Apocalyptic Mannequin

Underneath Atomic Lake

In a soup of neon-green waste,
the water, sharp to the touch, bubbled
like acid-filled blisters, each pop a face melt,
a boiled-down bone glowing in the night
like luminescent quicksand looking
for its next meal.

It speaks sometimes, quietly at dusk,
its voice a whisper, a hushed sentence spoken
between the lizards and the ghosts, their secrets
piercing like arrowheads raked across flesh,
strong enough to draw blood, all those red drops
like drowning berries, like bleeding hearts,
frolicking in the lake.

Sometimes I sit on its shores, watch it
as it feeds, all that sitting hunger, it eats
with abandon, never full, forever searching,
a toothless mouth that rips and tears, each bite
a sucking erasure, it slips off flesh like a winter jacket,
wraps its meat in atomic tongues, all those well-worn
muscles baked nuclear, it folds beneath radio waves
like static, dim and waiting, a soft, subtle glow.

The Survival of Fishes

There's a ship inside my stomach,
its sails set to drown, to crash and splinter
like the wood of the boats I sank, all those
men evaporated into shards, into rubble,
into dust.

> Tell me: do Krakens eat the souls of women
> who never wanted to be sirens?

Because I don't remember what it felt like
to breathe air, the gills in my neck a skin flap
of waterproof life, this the survival of fishes,
of ladies who can't smile without showing
their teeth, their knives, their songs.

Inside the waves, there are faces, waterlogged
hands, wrinkled and pruned, but not mine,
never mine. My skin, a metallic green mixed
with the silver of fish hooks, my eyes
the shimmering pearls of fossilized tears,
the mourning of disbelief.

Yet, inside the coral, the shells of my people wait,
here, the magic, the glamour of my kind. Watch
as I mystify, as I perform the seduction of the tide:
I give them a little, I take it back. I cut them
in half, I swallow them whole.

> I wonder: is there a hell made for the bones of
> girls who were stolen before their time? A fire
> for the water that burned what's left of my humanity?

The Amputator's Flesh Fry

Under the bridge, I brush my gills smooth,
smoke a red herring to ease the shakes.
The salt water in my eyes burns,
but I can't stop swimming in the waste,
the pustules on my lips screaming like a left pot
boiling on the stove.

I squeeze lemon in the cuts on my legs,
savor the taste of citrus and charred flesh.
The last time I ate meat, there were clouds
in my eyes, the scent of lighting like ground
pepper and electrocution, a bright light
against the crescent waves.

A cracked teapot holds my tongue while
a garbage fire burns in the corner, the ash
of yesterday's fires against the skeletons of
last year's mistakes. I smile as the meat chars
blacker now, pick chunks of fat from my teeth.

Future Mannequins on Display

When the sun rises, the plasticizing begins:
it happens first in the limbs, moves inward
to remove the sex, and then there is a stillness,
a numbness, a quiet undertaking as our tongues
shrivel, as our eyes dry out.

We are then carefully painted pink, our lips
the perfect shade of rain-soaked petals,
our brows lined black against the smooth
nude plastic of our flesh, but there is
no hair fastened to our heads, each strand
ripped out or shaved, the baldness of our skull
an easier fit for the gas mask fastened
to our face.

Dressed in boots and blood-caked jackets,
we are loaded into trucks, left in open fields
of fire and radiation, our memories erased,
stolen, our brains lobotomized into complacency,
our bodies boiled, meat pies baked and burned
for practice.

But we are the army, the decoys chosen
to withstand the blast. It is our sacrifice
that teaches them how to kill, how to
massacre in numbers, our limbs their markers,
our blood their scores.

Dead People Down Here

This is your last warning.

I've tried to help you, to let you know that
empty stomachs are more dangerous than
whatever is screaming outside in the dark,
that desperate parents will do anything
to feed their child, to provide warmth
regardless of what the blanket is made of.

If you keep walking, it's your own fault.

I can't tell you how many bones I've used
as forks, and if I tried to count the days
I've spent shaking underground, my arms
wrapped around skeletons, drinking rain water
from skulls, I would owe you a thousand stories
that ended in slit throats and cracked spines,
spiced meats and new dining sets.

Listen to the signs, take a leap of faith.

There's only one way to leave these woods
and it's not with your loved ones
wrapped safely in your arms. Instead,
it's in the throats and gullets of neighbors,
their lives more important than whatever
crosses they bear on their backs.

Abandonment

When the world ended, I hid my heart in the trunks
of abandoned cars, their backseats polluted with
scratchy blankets and plastic water bottles, discarded trash
and newspapers fifteen years old.

No one thought to look in empty cafes with coffee grinds
for ambience, in pastry shops with mold on the ceiling,
the stench of everything dying mixed in with the icing
of bear claws and tortes—

      but that's where I kept my trust, under pots and pans,
      beneath broken teacups and chipped saucers, the memory
      of caffeine and past conversations still sour on my tongue,
      all those leftover promises now curdled in my stomach.

I buried my fears in open graves void of caskets,
their previous inhabitants floating like sugar cubes
in rivers after the flood. I swept the anxiety of existing
beneath graveyard dirt and puddles made of tears,
wondered if the bodies missed eating nightmares
while they danced and drowned in rain.

Hope seemed like a fool's errand, so under the floorboards
of my mother's house, I wrote poetry to no one, left post-it notes
carved with my father's last words. My brother was a memory,
our relationship a panorama of childhood games and inside jokes,
all of them too painful to carry with me, but too precious to forget—

      so I wrapped them up in spilled laughter and birthday cards,
      kissed them with cracked lips and wrapped them in ribbons
      made of hair, each bow a reminder that it's all gone,
      that it's still going, that Earth wasn't the only thing God
      chose to abandon.

                                      The Apocalyptic Mannequin

Lost Highways

Bodies shuffling down the highway, headless corpses
littering the ground, the streets are filled with garbage,
both paper and human alike: an apocalypse of waste
rotting in the streets, all those amputated limbs
festering gangrene like mold on coffee grinds, wet,
coarse, the envy of every dehydrated mouth housing
sand instead of water.

The air around you tastes like sex, hot, sticky, chapped
like between your legs during the first wave of summer,
but it's blood down there, running down your thigh,
the scream lodged in your mouth formed in pain, in bullets,
all those wounds and cauterized flesh the new way to be
tattooed.

It's days before you find food, something you can chew,
swallow, keep down without puking. It's raw, still alive
when you bite into it, the look in its eyes a dying
preacher's sermon, but you keep tearing, teeth to flesh,
the meat a hot slug sliding down your throat. You cry,
but only for a minute, the bloat in your stomach a popped
balloon.

When night comes, you crawl into cars, disappear under
bridges, a quiet shadow sulking under ruins and radon,
you try to shrink, their footsteps loud, their wails like
banshees starved and crazed. You think you've survived,
but deep down inside, you know you're being hunted,
that this kind of living is all part of the game.

What They Left Behind

I tear down walls with my tongue,
each house a splintered memory,
a shadow filled with wooden shards,
these, the chapped lips of animals, the teeth
of what remains from the seas,
from dark skies cut open in the name
of science, all their emptiness still heavy,
still vibrating in the air.

Only What Could Be Carried

The house was haunted, not with ghosts
but there were messages and tea leaves
in its skeleton, it's framework the stories
of nights we slept huddled together,
the gun next to our heads, the fear
ripping through our stomachs like the
coyotes howling outside our window.

We knew it was time to leave, time to cry
when the bullets ran out, when the garden
was ravaged by animals, by man,
their mouths bleeding, their hands shaking,
a trail of rotted teeth and hoof prints
leading back into the woods like the
breadcrumbs we'd never eat again.

There wasn't room for anything but necessity:
no dolls, no wooden trains. I left behind
my grandmothers' jewelry, took my father's
hunting knife, the blade still stained rust from
skinning rabbits and deer, but I let each child
take a book, something to ease their minds,
to help them survive when the bludgeoning began,
when the axes covered ceilings and the teeth
bit down the door.

Those Little Sacrifices

He kept a bible in his car,
but I tattooed daggers on the inside of my thigh
and all those broken bottles in my mouth,
all those misshapen bruises and twice-swallowed vows?
They kept him hidden in my sores.

Sometimes when I walk through the crossroads,
I remember the handkerchief of fingernails buried in the city,
the way he stitched his wounds with dental floss
like some amateur punk rock song, raw and filthy,
a martyr desiring to be something clean.

When I think of that night, how the rain
smelled like seaweed, like spoiled fish
I pluck my eyelashes like flower petals,
stick them in my pocket next to his bones,
this dank fever dream projecting ghosts
like wilting lilies against the asphalt.

But I don't wonder if it was worth it, this bargain,
this selling out, because the sky looks like blood
drip-dropping in the smoke around my feet; it's warm,
like fire, but cold like his flesh, and I think he would
have wanted this, a reprieve from hunger, a dressing
for my wounds, all those little sacrifices each defining
how we love.

This, the Sound of Begging

The front wheel of the cart sticks,
a jagged twitch against sirens
warning children to get inside,
its blare a sharp horn slicing through
chemical fog, a knife through butter:
when was the last time we ate?

The grocery stores are picked over,
my television drawn on the wall
in black paint. In my pocket,
two shotgun shells breathe,
their stains an advertisement
of the last time I left to find water.

At the gate, the moans of beggars
wrap razor wire against flesh-tickled
bats, this the weapon of choice in
a holocaust void of humanity—
       the sight of cannibalized lips
       hidden in the cheesecloth
       I wrap around my daughter's eyes.

Trapped Inside

In a house with broken windows and bleeding scars,
it's the ripped-up hardwood, the peeling wallpaper
that hangs from dented walls like wrinkled flesh,
how the kitchen stained tea leaves and fire smells
like every dinner we never got to have, all those
smashed glasses and wasted liquor, I've smoked
cigarettes hoping the acid in my mouth would
catch fire and burn me to rubble,

but every room keeps me tethered to the earth,
all those memories of your voice, how it crawled
inside my chest, suffocated me with every word,
the warm blanket stuffed in my mouth the only
kindness you've ever shown, a black snake
inside the garden I've tended for 30 years, always
nurturing, forever killing,

and yet the look in your eyes spoke novels, each
blink a disappointment for everything I never was,
and this is the moment, scattered amongst
a rocking chair, a nursey, Dad holding his shotgun
to my face, when I think about the time the lights
turned off, how the city went silent, and for just one
second, everything seemed beautiful: all those dropping
bodies, all those screams that weren't mine. For once,
no one was looking at me, and I was a part of something
bigger, something coveted: our bloodshed all the same.

Cannibalized

There are no mirrors left in the house, all those broken reflections
scattered in the backyard, raindrops on glass, those little pieces of
me lost, much like the apple core in my stomach, the rusted screws
in my spine.

I can't remember what it was like when we used napkins, how we
dabbed delicate lace curtains on our mouths, no juice, no blood,
our skin clean and unstained, fresh and full as a wedding night,
we prayed before every meal.

But it's been weeks since I brushed my hair, the knots all but woven
into my scalp, the bugs nesting inside a constant buzzing in my ears,
all that humming, purring, sometimes I feel it in my mouth, my teeth
vibrating, itching.

> I want to pull them out:
> > but it's good to be a weapon,
> > to carry your silverware on your face.

Saudade

There is something missing,
a feeling of nostalgia, madness,
this sickness over something lost,
forgotten. My eyes are two swallows
flying toward a remembrance of home,
an essence of belonging somewhere
after it all caught fire, the scent of burning
still hot on my cheeks.

      Do you know my name? The one
      my mother gave me? I can't place
      her touch, her words, the way I'm sure
      she used to sing to me, a seraph with
      a voice made of dandelions and satin.

Everything seems cloudy here,
this road a pavement of loss; I watch
the shuffling feet of survivors—if surviving
is what we did—but the bleeding woes of
dismemberment, this infection of melancholy,
amnesia, it sits in my head, a weighted sorrow,
eating away at my memories: the first time I cried,
the boy with the softest lips, the way my grandmother
used to carry me in her arms.

      Can you help me? Is there safety
      in numbers? Will you hold my hand
      while I search for myself, while I rack
      the forest for a sign, anything that can
      tell me why I'm crying, whose child
      I'm carrying, why the sky looks like
      crows are carrying it on their backs…

A Collection of Pomegranate Seeds

An assortment of bones rests in my front yard
I can't remember the last time I watered the flowers,
they wilted, starved in a vase on the kitchen table,
their colors drained in pools of pink and white
on the linoleum floor.

The smell of coffee beans, like dirt, like burial,
fills the breath in my lungs, but I don't caffeinate
like I used to when the sun still came up. My body
feels different now, unused and stiff, the taste of
awakening on my tongue like fog after the rain.

There's a pile of packages on my doorstep,
a signature I'm unfamiliar with. In the distance,
I hear dogs barking, but I never see a beating heart,
just pomegranate seeds collecting in my sink.

Return to Sender

My stomach is a dirge of unopened letters
Lick the wax seal, tear into me with your tongue
I can't remember the last time someone read to me
or the way foreign words sound
tumbling off someone else's lips.

Behind my eyes, I hear the scrape of envelopes
All these fingernail clippings stuck in my throat
Do you feel the emptiness of forgotten signatures?
The unanswered proposals lingering on fingertips
stained by stamps and ink?

The weight of it gags me, this staunch repression,
this hidden doorway of truth.

It's been seven years since I've thought of you
The smell of your disease still rotting in my drawer
Tell me: when the sun disappears, will our notes cremate
with our ashes? Will the secrets we wrote, be but quiet
hauntings in our place?

The Apocalyptic Mannequin

Hospital Notes Written on the Gauze for My Sores

Stagnant, like the fly on my window
I wander these halls, a bodily repetition,
my limbs wrapped in the curse of age
the scent of hospice sheets on my tongue,
stale, poignant. Cement bags weighted
under my eyes.

The earth is gray,
a melancholic desert—
my orange juice is sour, my tongue
swollen with bite.

There is a happening inside my head,
twice, daily, they feed me pills; I hide them
under my bed next to the memory of my father's
voice. Mother hates my wheeze, my reflection
mourns behind the mirror.

I wonder if a diagnosis means prison,
a shackled existence with a sentence
to death.

The wallpaper peels off in love letters,
fills my hands with warnings, such sweet
songs of madness. Outside, the rain freezes,
an apocalyptic tear held frozen against
the message of time.

I Walk Nowhere in Cities Long Past Dead

In close quarters, a hunger spreads among us
infected and inhumane, we have the virus,
this anxious unknowing, this impending dread
it cripples the best of us, leaves the others hanging
from belt loops: faces swollen, eyes milky white,
their necks snapped, their jaws still moving.

I walk nowhere, the ghost of my sister beside me—
silent but screaming, the forest covets her secrets.
I hold the jacket I stole from her corpse, the smell
of her rotted flesh still lingering, a soured perfume
alongside the filth in these cities long-past dead.

Yet inside me, there's this gnawing, this growing
death-tick: it beats against the drum of my heart
the way my cell phone used to vibrate, but there's
no service in this abandonment, no gas, no electricity.

I checked the walls of the pharmacy. They were bare,
naked like the trees, empty like my stomach, their memory
a mockery to the life I once knew: all those names, that history,
strangled and erasing, forgotten in the carnage, lost in rivers
running red with blood.

Dinner Time: The Consequences of Savages

Breathe me the sound of teeth,
This moribund dream of cannibal proclivity,
I am the hunger that wakes you at night,
That clawing, the subtle mastication
That gnaws your eyes open to bleed

Feed me the songs of your gluttony
Let me listen to the dirge of your compunction,
How you feasted on hearts, a salacious monger
of wayward girls and ghost-driven women,
Your mouth is the centerpiece to my table.
        We eat at 8:00.

Do you like the depth of my depravity?
The scrape of your skin from the fork
Sliding against your skull?

Let me teach you how to sever, how to saw
Through sternums, through muscles made tight
From running. Mine is a penchant to punish,
To sauté the lack of emotion from your blood,
An effervescent bubbling, this first course
Of meals shared by sisters.

But don't worry, there will be more delicacies
To savor, an entire spread of wanton crimes,
All those forgotten offenses you butchered away
while starved from the pleasures of flesh. The taste
of you is acrid, a fetid spoil in my mouth.
        I'll devour you regardless.

But tell me, is the pressure too hot? Does the fire remind
You of the way you toasted their flesh, how you

Tattooed their memories with the removal of their
Bones?

For there are pairings of monsters, a silence
With no room left to scream. Look at me, this blossom
Of pertinence. I am made solely of teeth.

Cannibalism: A Robot Anachronism

I eat the parts of the robot dissections that can't be reused, won't be
refurbished; I build myself anew, a straggler, a vagabond, I scour the hazmat
tents and contamination labs, sort through the biohazard bags and junkyard
waste for in these carcasses are mechanisms, instruments: a fresh start, a
chance to reinvent and resurface amongst the others.

> *Just a pinch of technology,*
> *a dash of warfare...*

Give me its metal gears, its stray wheels, and broken cogs, the scraps of
aluminum that cut
my gums as I floss with stray cables, brush with burnt wire. Feed me their
automated hearts,
let me slurp oil from severed tongues, drink the phosphorus glow of
abandonment that only their copper eyes could have seen.

> *Just a sprinkle of radiation*
> *a dusting of extinction...*

Oh, look! Another one is dying: I can hear the tinkering, the wheezing death
of motorized lungs, the scratching clank of rusted limbs. Discard them, reject
them, I need this graveyard of engines, this boneyard where steam goes to
die. Tell me, what was human? What is machine? I am neither and both: my
master, ashamed.

> *A broken rule*
> *A disobedience*

We all exist to die.

From the Mouths of Plague-Mongers

I am the additional trash amongst the plastic bags and cigarette butts,
a malfunctioned doll in the science of reincarnation,
a hologram of stolen parts,
a human graveyard of misplacement
who stews in the alleyways of hospitals and morgues
gathering threads and body parts, needles and anesthesia
slurping the bone marrow from blood bags to stay alive.

> Cover your eyes.
> Don't look at me.

A cardiac catastrophe, a female miscarriage,
they told me I was beautiful, an extraordinary flower of rebirth,
but they plucked off my limbs like petals,
passed me around in a pollination orgy of stingers and honey,
drowning me in a hive of reproduction and abandonment
only to be cast out, orphaned along with the others,
the ripped and discarded, the stitched and disfigured.

> Leave now.
> Look away.

There's no help for the creatures we've become,
the plague-collectors, the disease-mongers,
we'll take your scraps, your unwanted flesh and fat,
we're hungry and cold, broken and lame,
we are the frankenwhores of society: aborted, bereaved,
and like the monsters that created us, we cannot die.

The Manufacturing of Bodies

Carbon copies on repeat, this in-and-out shuffle,
a delicate dance of blood serum and wires dipping,
turning, shifting, we mold to our masters, a blueprint
made of flesh and bone, here we chomp and chew
the words we've been told to say, pre-programed
to anticipate every want or need, an electronic brothel
at your fingertips, a buffet of bodies incapable of choice.

> *bend us to your will*
> *shape us to your preference*

We flock to assembly lines like salivating dogs,
desperate for upgrades, a new model, sleeker, thinner,
we wander like lost children, grabbing for perfection:
brighter eyes, a more inviting smile. Do we break
if we can't bleed? Each incision a recyclable scar,
all these scraps of metal, these strips of steel, they
wear on our hard drives in bruised memories, a collection
of electronic pain spread out in blurred pixels.

> *we still have life to give*
> *we can still participate*

But it's dark behind the delete key, an inkjet
ocean of spilled expectations, empty pages and
unopened browsers, our livelihood a screenshot
in your life, a forgotten story on your feed,
no likes, no reactions, just silence, a footprint
in a system built to abandon, to forget.

> *Please hit copy*
> *hit copy*
> *hit copy*

> paste.

The Apocalyptic Mannequin

Inside this pile of broken glass
On the edge of splintered wood,
Call my name against the drip-drop of rain on tin,
To the tune of metal grindings and radiation screams;
    Wind me clockwise until I start to breathe,
    Scoop out the dust in my macramé lungs,
    Help me, I'm dead but I'm dying again,
    A tortured corpse amongst this toxic waste:

        …they named me disappearance
        …baptized me, withering,

Still, between the stones that collect in the pits of my eyes
I wilt to the smell of rot and gun smoke,
Cringe at the sound of human consumption,
The tattoo of my ancestor's serial numbers
Burned into my once-blushed cheeks now stained ashen in their memory;
    Please, paint me in the picture of what was once human
    Cast me in flesh, build me with skin and bone
    There's death in this camp of dystopian nightmare
    A plague house filled with bodies made of dreams:

        …they stripped me naked
        …burned me to plastic.

At the Neon Circus

Stuffed inside a cello case at the neon circus,
the technicolor glow of chipped face paint caught my eye,
reminded me of red and white tents and cotton candy holograms,
of hallucinatory harmonics and mechanique ballets,
but trapped inside this clockwork catastrophe, this industrial imprisonment,
I twitch, I malfunction, I short-circuit in freak-show electrocution,
Too excited at the prospect of dancers, at the idea of animatronic musicians
Returning to play with me once again,
        but no one ever comes and yet still I pluck my own strings
        a solo-performer auto programmed to self-destruct,
my left eye blinking, my right eye stagnant, sealed shut from
low ticket sales and poor attendance, a forever artist, starving, thirsty...

I scratch the leather case, my steel fingernails a thorn in the upholstery,
wonder what it would be like to oil my lungs, to sing hypnosis again,
to belt out those automatic musings programmed in my head—
        the ones that don't stop,
        the ones that repeat,
            forever playing

                over and over and over again...

Yes, these fever dreams of opera! These salt mines of un-cried tears!
I tune myself to the sound of bombings, to the sad wails of Italian poets,
to the weary stares of painters with cubist faces scarred by seismic ruin,
but the countdown to my annihilation wears taut against my routine
and bound by my master's hand, I die to save art, to save humans:
listen to me, silent. Play me, loud.

        I never wanted to stop
        I always wanted to play
            forever performing

                over and over and over again.

All Things Poison

The mannequin on my shelf is bleeding, its head
the resting place for snakes. Sometimes when I look at it,
I feel like rubbing mandrake on my skin, letting its toxins
sink into my flesh the way your body fell into the grave,
soft and sudden like how Luna moths appear, their wings
like silk blankets shining in the light.

It's intoxicating, the way it looks like you: stiff and pale,
waiting and silent, a cluttered air that drips in corners,
the kind that no amount of smoke can cleanse, and so
I started to take my tea with Wolfsbane and Vervain,
lick Foxglove petals from my lips, each sip a seizure,
every swallow a separate prayer.

And tonight, the moon is red, this walk my death march
toward the shadows in its eyes, but my breath doesn't falter,
the taste of all things poison pumping through my blood,
each pulse an aphrodisiac, a way to touch what's left of
crime and passion, the accumulation of human mirage,
but this plastic photograph is a sleight of hand, this night
a hallucination, and no matter how much sorrow I mix
with the onset of death, it's something even magic can't undo.

Marionette Disorder

When I step on the scale, the wood in my stomach
leaves splinters in my mouth. I am made of pine,
painted red with rouge, with cherry-stained marks,
they call me woman, but I am not my reflection,
my body unknown to the insects breeding inside
the pocket of my coat

> *I weigh termites and rotten bagels,*
> *leftover Chinese food and maggots.*

In an effort to leave my skin, I scrape wood shavings
off my head, polish the marbles of my eyes,
an intimate act that fools not even the strings
attached to my arms, even my heart doesn't beat,
its likelihood filled with foam chips and sawdust.

> *I vomit fruit flies and applause,*
> *children's laughter and freshly spun cocoons.*

On my shelf, I linger, a fainted effigy, a collapsed
lung, my shirt too tight, too itchy, my necklace
a silver handcuff, my own personal restraint
locking me in this performance piece, my lips
never moving, my voice, not my own.

> *I starve myself unhinged, my collapse*
> *a punchline, the climax of the show.*

The Mannequin Legs on My Bed

Loneliness sits next to the mannequin legs on my bed,
they're crossed because I like to imagine the outline
of a lady, someone refined and worthy of my respect.

But on the days when it's hard to breathe outside,
I like to dress her in mosquito net, a salacious attempt
to imagine a willing whore at the foot of my bed.

The nights are eternal now, the absence of touch
a too-present reality. I cut a hole in the space
between her thighs, tell myself that it's as good
as the real thing.

Yet outside, the wind moans louder than any sound
I've heard from the bed, the creaks of old springs
the key holder to my fantasy, a quiet judgment
whispered to an empty silhouette.

Walking on Teeth: A Memoir

The morning rays of light ease across the garden,
the grass freshly kissed with ash, a charcoal stain
lingering on the lips of dried flowers and bones.

I've learned to tiptoe, to walk on eggshells and glass,
for here on the dirt floors of abandoned shacks
sleep the corpses of roaches, the bodies of faceless children,
their clothes the mulch of monsters who frequent these hidden streets,
their stomachs the rumblings of volcanoes, their fleshy scales
the delicate lace of a dying mosquito's wings.

Sometimes I watch behind the skeleton trees, my pockets
full of witch stones and twigs, the chants of my ancestors
still hot on my tongue. Their arrival is a torrent
of screams, their hunger thick like molasses,
like blood and honey dripping from my ears.

If I count to ten, I can feel their hate pulsating in the air,
the stench of rotted wounds, of broken alliances
and shattered families the only stories carved into tree bark,
into slabs of broken concrete on the ground. Promise me
you'll walk carefully into the teeth, into the knives
of a new race of gods, for this memoir of suffering, of hidden
footsteps and lost translations are the only warnings left
for the babies abandoned, crying in the woods.

Our Room of Walking Coffins

Quiet is the still of night
Wrapped in blankets of cobwebs:
Their silk strings the bandana
Across my mouth, their larvae,
My moving lips.

Let's wade through this sepulcher
Of white, this our eight-legged ballad,
Be mindful of the scurry of shadows,
The elegy of squeals written in the stones.

Can I invite you to our room of walking coffins?
My pillow is stuffed with egg-sack sachets,
The bulbous movement of their children a
Nightmarish massage, my throat a raw pink
From all the screams.

Yes, sleep well, my child, here in this den of
Soporific swells. Drink from the veins of our
Torpid bodies, extract the saturnine fluids
From our yellowed eyes. This death dance of
Dejected faith flows through our legs in
Arachnophobic quakes. Close your eyes
To the tortuous spinning. Here, we are destined
To corpse.

Wayward Spirits of Dreams and Sand

We slept like the porcelain dolls of children:
our eyes shut, cemented with spider webs
and the fingerprints of shadows, our coffins
the birth blankets of stillborn babes. The bags
under our eyes held a century's worth
of nightmares, the hair on the floor a dusting
of scalp pulled from our own heads.

If you listen, the scratching of our heartbeat
mixes with the breathing of your dreams, each
fear, Morpheus's climax, every prayer, his
private exorcism. Be still when you taste the air
of this somnambulist waltz. It is a diary
of faded memories and mismatched murders,
this the hypnosis, the witchcraft of subconscious wants.

But like skullcap paste, we'll relax your muscles,
our whispers an ounce of freshly harvested valerian root
stuck deep inside your ears; can you hear us humming,
buzzing, drilling these clouds inside you? We will hang
your eyelids out to dry, drink the water that dribbles
from your mouth. We are the children stuck between
veils, the wayward spirits of sand: beware our kiss.

Mirror Gazing

"Hell is empty / and all the devils are here."

—Shakespeare, *The Tempest*

In front of the mirror, the voices of shadows
spoke to me in subtle horrors, their howlings
like a lover's moans, scared but wanting,
all those desires, those murderous thoughts—
the way I ripped off eyelids, dressed chapped
lips with nails, dug piercings into bones—they slipped
through the reflection like smoke, like confessions,
like tear drops on quartz, a champagne suicide,
oh, how I drank them down: bitter as a new moon,
stubborn as a wolf.

The hours passed like cricket songs in its presence,
my body a mirage, the way it took up space
like a canyon, so full and empty, it swallowed
wishes the way ghosts eat through walls
and when I reached out, tried to grab my own hand,
blood dripped from the corners, a slow dribble
of crimson black, my lips against the glass:
licking, tasting, desperately lapping—

It filled me red, sucked the air from the room,
my body heaving, back arched, muscles tight,
all those whispering whimpers, those delicate devils,
singing, praying, begging me to let them out, all those
sweet little souls with talons and split tongues, their eyes
like snake venom and oil, a vision of Death and all
its promises seeping into my open arms, dressing me
in darkness, bathing me in sin.

They rushed me like a disease, like a cancer
that'd spread through my blood, thick and heavy,
rancid and rotted, I spit up gravel and ashes, choked
on fingernails and hair, and around me, everything
quieted, a slow burn, a steady massacre, the fate of the
world on the hinge of their first scream.

Of Sleeping Witches Woken

Close me off with a wicker broom,
these words, an eclipse of the last time
vultures wept, all the sunlight gone,
the echoes of gun chambers still reverberating
in the wind against my hand.

The song of charred bones hangs in the air,
this the melody of scavenging, of lost limbs,
forgotten lore. If there was a Goddess,
she's since been devoured, the tongue of her ancestors
ripped out and burned, an offering to darkness,
to the shadows that make homes inside us all.

In the forest, the rain falls upward, a signature,
these reverse angel wings. Speak softly:
should the earth swallow your words,
payment is to be taken. Beware the consequences
of a fire too bright, of sleeping witches woken.

For I Am a Woman Made of Snakes

The rage in my womb is beating against the concrete,
the taste of blood, like metal, like cherries, bleeding
against my teeth. I feel myself rip-rip-ripping,
the massacre of my flesh poised against a toddler
tearing a drawing of his mother.

Off go her legs
Off go her arms

A crow stands staring at me, its head cocked, curious,
the glimmer of its black beak shining against the
pool of blood at my waist. Inside, there is a pulsing,
an echo of remorse, a last breath choked against
apologetic whispers.

There goes its chance
There goes its future
At the window, the snake is hissing against the glass,
its saliva the salve I need to glue myself together,
to husband stitch my way to new beginnings, to paper dolls,
to puzzle pieces.

I exist to kill my children
just so he can eat.

The Stones They Threw

Trapped under the wreckage, I am the swept,
the dirt collecting under the rug. Should a footstep
find itself lodged in my throat, the silenced screams
of my stillborn sisters will ring in a new year of
burning Sabbaths, the stones cast the very weight
needed to bring their oppressors down.

Inside the House of Labor

In this house, the scrapes and screams of life can be heard,
each bellow a rib-breaking shriek, the slap of blood on thighs
like wet bird feathers coasting through storms. The breeders
weep, their moans a suffocating wail while girls crawl out
from their holes, hungry and suffering, their death sentences
stamped at the moment of their birth

but on beds made of straw, these women beg to be killed,
their bodies unwelcomed strangers, a skin sack filled with
eggs and pain. They are the natural companions to death, their
wombs sacrificed in a political addendum, a contract for life
in exchange for the next generation of wombs.

What Mother Couldn't Tell You

Bedridden and bleeding, my stomach swollen
like a bruised balloon, I swallow instructions
on how to survive, a dying mother's manual
on creatures and contagions, on dissection
and mutation, a last attempt to pass on
my knowledge, a desperate attempt to
keep my child alive.

From Maiden to Monster

At the foot of my bed, there was a growling,
a snarl that was half-human, half-wolf, a mongrel
with one golden eye, one red—crimson as a blood moon,
its breath like wet earth and copper, damp on my legs.

I tried to hide, to wish myself invisible, but its hands
were more like claws that were more like knives, sharp
and slick, a smile of starvation painted across its lips,
this air of desperation, of hunger suddenly palpable
in the air we both breathed.

When it held me down, its body like a casket, a tomb
built perfectly for me, my limbs went stiff, went marble
as I turned into a statue carved by fear, everything tight,
everything blurring, the glint of its teeth like a flashlight
shining in my eyes.

It smelled like pine needles kissed with rot, like leaves
scattered in stagnant water, the scent of all things dying
but fighting to live clinging to its tongue the way our skin
settles around our bones.

And like velvet, it slid across me, the brush of its fur
a mourning dress, the touch of its pelt the lining to my
casket, this a blanket made of insects and dirt.

It wasn't long before my flesh dressed its face, a mask
made of maidens long-past gone. I sat next to my sisters,
this monster our debutante ball, the closest we'd get
to finding a suitor, our stories written, our fate sealed,
our dripping blood the ball gown of our dreams.

Stephanie M. Wytovich

Scavenger

The feathers on my face are coated nuclear,
the brush of excrement a step I've since
adopted to my morning routine. I sit, hungry,
my short neck a bent spoon, my back hunched,
a dark cape against the backdrop of the rain:
is it too soon to be starving? To feel this raging
pit inside my chest?

At noon, I sweep the roads, seek out the perfume
of death, my version of a gourmet dinner, all those
bloated bodies sinking, decaying in the streets; it's
like a smorgasbord of infection, a piñata filled with
maggots and disease.

For a moment, I try to remember a time
when my beak wasn't bloody, wasn't lodged
deep in the throats, in the stomachs of family,
the intestines of friends, but I stretch my wings,
my talons manicured, my beady eyes sharpened,
the taste of all things lifeless the bullseye as I dive.

The Apocalyptic Mannequin

Woman Meat

Cut me open and I bleed, yes, I gush like mountains,
my red rivers like pomegranate surrender, each drop,
every seed, a step closer to entrapment, this my isolation,
the scarlet letter etched in my womb.

Sometimes I wonder if it's possible to hold it all in,
this scream, this agony, how it builds inside, bursting
like waterfalls, the afterbirth of my rage carried away
by cardinals, their wings an open slaughter in the sky.

Yet here I lay beneath tents made of my flesh, a stuck pig
writing her eulogy, the earth drinking my butchery like
a fine wine with notes of cherry and murder, their hunt
still on, the women still hiding, running, cowering
in shadows meant only as blankets for themselves.

And it's nightfall before I hear the fire, the crackle
and spit of flames, the sweet musk of smoke amidst
hungry mouths ripping and tearing at my meat, this
savagery the death of body, the beginning of our curse.

Still Life with Scars

There are knife wounds across my chest, the whisper
of a bullet on my arm. If you can get past the cracked
bones, the way my teeth hang at an angle, you'll see
I am a still-life trauma dressed in scar tissue, a forest
of bound fractures, a storm of smoke-damaged lungs
coughing on curfews, the echoes of active shooters
still ringing in my ears.

But if you say my name, I'll bleed apologies
like a butcher's block, each plea a watercolor portrait
dressed in tendons and tears, every prayer a gaslit hiccup
washed down with the stale communion wine of
empty churches; I still trip on their promises, on all those
corpses with eyes that look like his.

You see, it's not enough that I survived, that my life
is a reel of stained-glass memories, of sandstorm bombings,
the taste of metal in the air, but rather it's how the tourniquets
on my wrists are still weeping, how the thorns in my scalp dig
deeper, my face dressed with pain, this descent, this crucifixion,
there's no such thing as death if there's no one left to watch
you die.

As the Crow Flies

In a chair next to a window, there is a girl,
a shadow, a wilting orchid. When no one
is looking, a petal drops, a rib pokes out,
a flutter of wings hits the glass like bodies
on pavement: the sound expanding, growing,
blossoming like cancer until it stops breathing,
the emptiness a pressed crow, a tarred feather,
all those little feelings marinating inside her
like grinding teeth and blood clots, the crowded
room now filled with nothing but ghosts.

Identification

I identify as haunted,
as a broken violin,
a forest wrapped in fog.

If you look between my legs,
you will find an empty library,
each shelf a collection of ghostings,
blank signage for a dimly light hallway,
a spider web, an unfinished opera.

I am neither a baptism dress
nor a wedding ring, a wake photograph
nor a satin-lined bed. If you call,
I will not answer, if you run,
I promise to hide.

But inside my chest beats a jewelry box
with no sound, walks an orphan forever
flipping pages of an unwritten book.

If you pick up the rose on the table,
or smell the salts stuffed into my mouth,
you'll find my future in my palms, my past
written in burn marks on my back.

Just wrap your wounds carefully,
for I am a host of century-lost diseases,
an epidemic, a long-forgotten plague, and if you
hold a seashell up to your ear,
it will whisper the endings to every poem,
my signature a cockroach, the poison
you left out for the rats.

The Apocalyptic Mannequin

Call Me Haunted

My eyes are brown, but sometimes they go black,
black like crow feathers, like the still-burning wax
drying on your letter. It's like they're two pools
of obsidian water, my face its own scrying mirror,
these memories and nightmares as clear
as the moon water I soak in, each night a baptism,
every day its own drowning.

But the poison in my veins grows belladonna
beneath my nails, nightshade between my ears,
an apocalyptic love letter dressed in purple greens—
I am both deadly and beautiful, the perfume
of my skin an intoxicating blend of Hecate's
breath dripping warmth down my neck.

Yet it's this steady ticking of heartbeats,
all these broken clocks screaming, pulling tight
inside my bones. I am stretched and hurting, my blood
thinning, cooling, a cracked window, a rotted framework,
these ghastly separations, these little evil spills,
they're like brick dust blowing curses in my whispers,
like red pepper slipping hexes in my prayers.

Can you hear them? Their voices like sulfur
dripped in clover, smooth yet vile, all this burning,
this heat around my feet. It's loud and it's growing,
tie my wrists behind my back, stuff a rag inside my mouth,
there's no telling what scars my body still bears, what stories
are still left to be told. I am both death shroud and newborn babe:
they call me haunted, and they're not wrong.

Return to Womb

Pickpocket dinners stolen from fast food chains
this sound of lavender against the fan
she is the butterfly monger of trauma victims
a heroine drip stolen at dawn.

If you listen, you can still hear her breathe,
the steady wheeze of cigarette smoke built
up in her lungs, this bone cage rattle of cancer
eating her health like candy, a symphony of
wails.

Her house on 78th Street remains empty, a cavern of desiccated
haunts. In the bedroom, the daffodils are wilted, their yellow
wax sealed into the same carpet she burned at sixteen,
the suicide trance a genetic curveball she beat
into the floorboards, her knuckles bloody,
her muscles, torn.

But still, there are spirits in the walls
they float like silver balloons into the eye sockets
of moth-eaten dolls, such soft murder in memory
of the night she first ate her pain, sautéed it up like
newborn veal, her skin a host of spices and ash.

Too often, she walks the halls, leaves scratch marks
in the floral wallpaper. stick-figure drawings in the brick.
There is a dusting of eyelashes on the windowsill,
a jar of teeth in the bathroom cabinet. Can you hear the
echo of the return to womb? This collection of dismemberment
won't be left behind.

The Apocalyptic Mannequin

Corpse-Covered Glasses

The quake of the squall brought with it
a hailstorm of bodies, each one twisted,
turned, some inside out, their intestines
wrapped around their throats like leashes.

They dropped from the sky, each one its own
blood bomb, a meat bag of contagion. Hear me:
there was no escape from the explosion, each bone
a knife, a weapon hidden amongst the smog.

With corpse-covered glasses, I walked the streets,
the tingle of trauma still fresh in my spine. The trees,
each a branch-sewn net, collected limbs, heartbeats,
an organic basket for the mutilation pouring
from the skies like tomato juice, grapefruits.

This happened for three days once a year, always
in the summer, the stench of decomposition now an
earth-soaked perfume. The sounds of smacks and shatters,
crunches and caws sent people underground, buried,
the safest place a mockery of death at the dying season
happening above.

Λ Spectacle of Corpses

Usher me to the corpse room, the autopsy arena,
to the glass windows, the white, white walls,
give me sterility against a backdrop of flesh,
a moment to breathe in the passing of a soul.

I am here to witness life, take my number,
this line a moving wake of passing families,
of children eating pastries, vendors bathed
in powdered sugar, the scent of fresh apples
against a capitalist society, a whore turning tricks
to see the nameless bodies, the quiet johns all
tucked in and decomposing behind the next door.

My heart beats with a hangman's fear, this the
moment of watching, the striptease of the morgue.
Let me taste the quarters on your eyes,
how the stench of your hair mixes with the
perfume rubbed hastily into your skin. Feel it inside:
there's a pulsing in the air, this the spectacle of corpses.
I wonder if they feel pretty dressed up in oils and wax.

The Collection Day Saints

Beneath the gallows, the earth is warm with want,
the shadow of death a pendulum, a memento mori
for the bystanders who cheer to the last gasp,
their words a forced lullaby to the reaper, to the man
who shuffles souls into the next life.

But not me. I am neither Charon nor the executioner,
not the autopsy table nor the dead-man's judge. Here,
the skeleton of man stands tall, and I am the robber,
the thief of bodies and bones, a collector of flesh
not buried six-feet deep, the pallor of their faces
a pay check, an overdue bar tab. I cash them in:
eye for eye, tooth for tooth, their limbs a host of
mortgage payments, my family's produce for the week.

Don't ask me if I sleep at night, the echoes of
my shovel still too loud in my head. I don't see
the stars anymore, just blinking eyes, mud-covered
diamonds. There's no solace when the sun goes down,
just a battle of filth and rigor mortis, a backache,
a sprained ankle, all tied with the hangman's noose,
their bodies piled like rapture-day presents, their necks
snapped, faces toward the heavens. I almost feel bad,
but even the dead must do their jobs, and people like me,
we're known as the harbingers, the collection day saints.

Consumption's Footprint

The air is washed with blood, a red fog that hangs
like a dead man's sneeze. Suffer them softly,
these the children who bathe in the woods, the ageless,
the immortal, their clothes sullied by murder, their handkerchiefs
filled with consumption's footprint. It is they who breathe
the stench of leeches and madmen, meat and fresh wounds;
their tongues, a pulsating hunger, a new moon suicide
to cleanse the ache, the energy of a freshly made corpse.

See how they walk, their limbs broken twigs, their nails
yellowed, brittle, their teeth scattering the forest floor
like acid rain. What was once human, is now a festering scab,
an infected carcass, the eyes two pits of stitched and swollen
sores. Listen to them howl, how they cry during the night, a constant
begging to be saved, to be cured… to be fed.

But it's what's inside them, that hurts. The poisoning, bludgeoning,
how their veins leak and their arteries curdle, each cough
a death sentence, every hack a crushing blow to weeping lungs;
sometimes when it's quiet, you can hear them bleed—
the steady stream of death louder than even the most
soul-sucking of screams.

Gather the Townspeople

At the last sound of death, the townspeople gathered,
their presence a prayer, a group séance to help assist
the corpse, to cleanse the spirit, make it new.

They took turns holding the body, cradling it like a child,
each member dousing themselves in baptismal water, their flesh
soaking, sopping along with the dead's, this the practice of washing,
of mourning, of confronting the lines drawn by mortality
in the river of our tears.

With careful ease, they dried the skin, hugged the shoulders
in a farewell's embrace, shrouded the body in fine linens,
these the soft-kept blankets mothers buried after birth.

Outside, the people chanted mantras of safety, the guiding lyrics
of eulogies and dreamlike woes, each voice a soothsayer,
every song the refrain to death's final words, a poem to the heavens,
an aria to the gatekeeper, and if you listen carefully, sometimes
the soul sings, too, when it finally decides to leave.

The Midwives of Death

At the bedside of the infected, a symphony of black,
of pressed shadows and flowing echoes, stand the
midwives of death: the assistant reapers who birth
hushed voices and red-rimmed eyes while the room
collects final words, bandages trimmed black with blood.

When they come, their presence, like a fluttering of bats,
like the gentle wisp of spider legs on arms, they sing
the songs of grief and despair, their voices the scalpel
to weeping flesh, to stitched-up scars, those forgotten wounds,
the mismatched agonies we've spent years trying to hide.

If we call to them, they'll drink our spirits, reach deep
into the idea of what we call life, twist our ancestral
fingerprints until our names become our last identifiers,
the signature we can no longer sign as our souls swim
with the waves of yesteryear, ride the hurricanes of grave
markers and freshly tossed dirt.

They're both the chauffeur and the hearse, the morphine
and the coding, and if we search for the sounds of violins
and trumpets, for notes left by jazz musicians in underworlds
and purgatories, paradises and heavens, we find onyx eyes
and burning sage, the rhythm of bay leaf wishes and canopic jars,
for these are the women who conduct the rites of mourning,
who play the orchestra of our last words, conduct the operas
of our sufferings.

It is they who sing us back to sleep, who feast on the spoils
of souls, each mark a sin devoured, a wickedness erased,
and before the last star cries out in winter, before we're tucked
into our caskets wearing our Sunday best, there won't be time
to beg nor plead, to reason with or bargain; it will just be us
and the women, the scythe and the tears, our judgements open
to the fates, not a single moment left to ask when or why.

The Apocalyptic Mannequin

Dear Santa Muerte

In halls painted by marigold petals,
a skull sits in the corner, the scent
of ganja in the air while tequila
is dribbled down the remains of its mouth,
an offering for protection, this the holy tribute
to the goddess of death, the maiden of change,
of transformation, her smirk the flesh of drunk men
kissed in bars, of curious hands run across
a woman's full breasts

> *Escuchame grandes diosas*
> *Te ruego a tus pies*

On my knees, I crawl, your likelihood
a pendent on my neck, this the pilgrimage
to heal broken spirits and shattered bones,
the fire of my prayer still hot on my tongue,
burning, bleeding, the scar of my past,
the weight of my sorrows, I submit them
to you like effigies of my suicides,
like portraits of my bile-stained coughs.

> *Protegeme, dulce muerte*
> *Envuelveme en tu abrazo*

I pluck strawberries off their vines, eat
the sugared icing off pastries at the store,
anything to replace the soured taste
of stale beer and pills, the memories
of bullet holes, the poetry of unattended
wounds, all of this, the ghosts of my existence,
the incubi of my nights, all those harrowed wailings,
those defenseless silent screams.

Por favor…ayudame
Mi vida esta en tus manos

Corpse Meditation

Convinced of our immortality, we walk the earth
scavengers of flesh and bone, the quiet deaths
of man and animal an unfazed reality until it touches
our lives, breaks into our homes, sleeps in our beds,
the subtle breath of decomposition now the whispers
we hear before falling asleep.

It rots in our brains, this concept of death, of expiration,
our fears distended, ruptured at the putrefaction of
the world, how it bloats and sags, cries and suffers, the skies
a layer of smoke, the oceans a graveyard of mutations, all these
discolored visions of who we used to be now masked
against the desiccated corpses of who we've become.

Do you take part in the dismemberment, in the consumption
of a shallow grave and a wooden cross, your name but a bone
rattle away from being forgotten, churned to dust? Can you
push aside the shadow of the reaper, the metallic lure
of white lights and sudden regrets, the untraveled roads and
scores of mismatched company?

Because in the end, it comes for us, it comes for us all,
wings spread, mouth open, the stench of echoes
and silence all but a memory in our hearts.

The Martyrdom of Saints

Crippled limbs against stone walls
breathe the musk of sacrifice, of money
spent to sleep next to saints, the crisp allure
of decomposing flesh amongst decaying
martyrs now the city's most attractive trend.

Outside, the bodies collect, the corpses stacked
in holes made of death and disease. They are
the infected, the poor, the unfortunates who
danced in the graveyard, screaming to the skies,
dirt in their hands, blood in their teeth,
the desperation of redemption a pack instinct,
all this hunger ripping through their veins.

The hangman's noose appears and the executioner
smiles. Ropes fasten wrists and ankles, the mud
a splish-slosh of failed runaways and rebellions,
the ache of yearning, of being kept away from
heaven too much, all these broken necks and
lifeless wombs now the subject of children's
ghost stories, the hollowed shadows that still
go bump in the night, that still try to dig their
way out of the hell around them.

The Apocalyptic Mannequin

I Bury Them Screaming

Illness dressed their faces, those blood-stained smiles,
all those glassed-over eyes, it took months of practice,
steady hands, a strong stomach, but now I can walk
past fields of corpses, inside pyramids of bodies, my
mask a plague doctor's dream as I sniff out survivors,
all those lucky enough to wear death as an accessory
instead of a tattoo.

Usually they smell sweet, their sweat like lemongrass
amongst a canopy fear, yet the ground sings lullabies
to their feet, lures them down into the earth, a dirt blanket
made of worms and shattered glass, I bury them screaming,
pour gravel down their throats, their pleas almost biblical,
each breath a prayer, every gasp a sermon, but it's not
my responsibility to play God, for I am the caretaker,
and this new Eden is my garden.

Open Casket

My face mask is spattered with unspoken words,
my mouth thick, heavy with letters I've written
and will never deliver, the plague doctor behind
my eyes a sealed envelope, its contents the secret
visions hanging like mist above my head.

I rub red wax out of the corner of my eyes, the
skeletons of my thoughts dancing on bare tables,
the fruits of my labor surrendered to maggots,
to the conqueror worms slipping inside my mouth,
all those fallen stars and empty graves, I taste like
coffin nails and rosemary trying to remember
my promise to you.

But it's getting colder now, the coins on my eyes
removed and spent, the garlic in my throat
breaking down the gases in my stomach, my blood
tainted, undrinkable like the sour grapes of bad
homemade wine, and I broke off my nails writing
poetry to you, each shard of wood in my finger
another stake through my corpse, my body
forever screaming, you deaf to my pleas.

Death Bed

My death bed is loose dirt and broken glass,
no one thought to give me better, just a symphony
of bruised organs and gravel in my throat, an ensemble
of broken nails and loose teeth, my tongue swallowed,
a sandpaper bulge cocooned in my throat.

There are twigs intertwined in my hair, dancing
among the maggots that form a wiggling crown,
their smooth bodies slipping along wet, matted hair,
the wind a sorry conditioner for split ends painted
with coagulated blood and sweat.

I didn't think to bring a blanket when I died, forgot
to fashion a pillow for my skull, my chapped skin
now burnt red, frostbit from the cold, the bloat
my only protection from the snapping mouths,
all those hungry teeth, gnawing through the forest,
searching for fresh death like a slaughterhouse whore.

But I am spoken for, my body a leaking faucet,
a slow coffee drip, each drop a drink for the earth,
corpse the main meal on the menu: please eat me
slowly, savor the rotted skin, lick out the week-old
marrow. I want to be touched one final time, devoured
like the goddess I used to be.

Eating What's Left of My Death

The world has shifted, its balance off, each blink
revealing a permanent blur, and it's no wonder
the crows scratching at my eyes want out, and I
can't blame the tentacles in my mouth for refusing
to hold water, but the moon can't be drawn down anymore
and the voices have quieted, disappeared amongst the trees,
all the swallows dropping from the sky like fresh ghosts
dipped in sealing wax.

I wonder: can you blindfold me, please? I need to focus
on the smell of cypress, swallow birch to reincarnate
the spirit of what's left. I take off my shoes, my feet deep
in the bile of the earth, all that mud and bone squishing
between my toes. I like the wet, feel comfortable in
the sludge, the conqueror worm inside me now, eating
what's left of my death.

Λ Masquerade of Reapers

Like black waves, an accidental spill of ink
they moved through the room like little horrors,
a creeping shadow on ceilings and floors, the face
of broken teacups and unanswered letters, they dipped,
they spun, each movement a step closer to caskets,
to headstones, another breath stolen from like-minds
and sleeping babes.

They partner unwillingly, reaching for hands like
needles in the dark, each prick a hallucination,
every stab a stolen kiss between friends. There's no
laughter around the staircase, no whispers in the walls,
but if you get close enough to feel the air between their robes,
to taste the wilted flowers staining their hands, the scythe
almost feels like dripping pearls against your neck, all these
quiet little screams wrapping your rib cage in stars.

It's not fast, but it's enough to feel like flying,
like holding a butterfly in your hands, its wings
thrashing against your palms, a heart beat, a tear drop,
if you close your eyes, they'll all dance with you,
dress you up like princesses and kings, like headless
queens and poisoned princes: just feel the beat and relax,
they'll count you in when you look ready.

About the Author

Stephanie M. Wytovich is an American poet, novelist, and essayist. Her work has been showcased in numerous anthologies such as *Gutted: Beautiful Horror Stories, Fantastic Tales of Terror, Year's Best Hardcore Horror: Volume 2, The Best Horror of the Year: Volume 8,* as well as many others.

Wytovich is the Poetry Editor for Raw Dog Screaming Press, an adjunct at Western Connecticut State University, Southern New Hampshire University, and Point Park University, and a mentor with Crystal Lake Publishing. She is a member of the Science Fiction Poetry Association, an active member of the Horror Writers Association, and a graduate of Seton Hill University's MFA program for Writing Popular Fiction. Her Bram Stoker Award-winning poetry collection, *Brothel,* earned a home with Raw Dog Screaming Press alongside *Hysteria: A Collection of Madness, Mourning Jewelry, An Exorcism of Angels,* and *Sheet Music to My Acoustic Nightmare.* Her debut novel, *The Eighth,* is published with Dark Regions Press.

Follow Wytovich on her blog at http://stephaniewytovich.blogspot.com/ and on twitter @SWytovich.